ISBN: 978-0692105412

Nannee and Grandpop

Thank you for always believing in me and fostering the growth of my imagination.

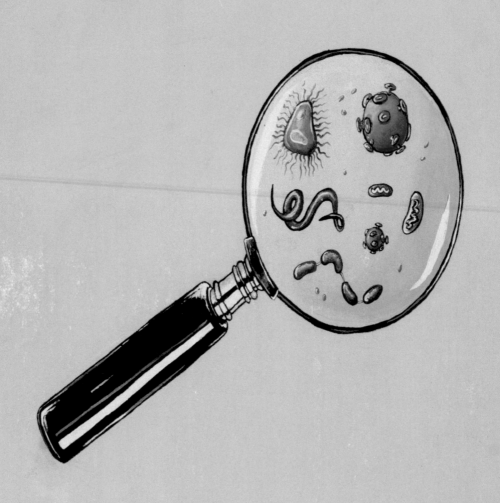

Germs are Yuck! Germs are Ick!

Germs cannot be seen but could make you sick.

Be careful what you touch
during the day,
you may get germs along
the way.

Germs can be on books and on toys.

Germs can be on the hands of other little girls and boys.

Don't put your fingers in your nose.

Don't wipe dirty hands on your clothes.

Keep your hands to yourself. Be caring.

Remember germs are not for sharing.

Always cover your nose before you sneeze.

Cough into your elbow please.

Washing your hands often everyday keeps those pesky germs away.

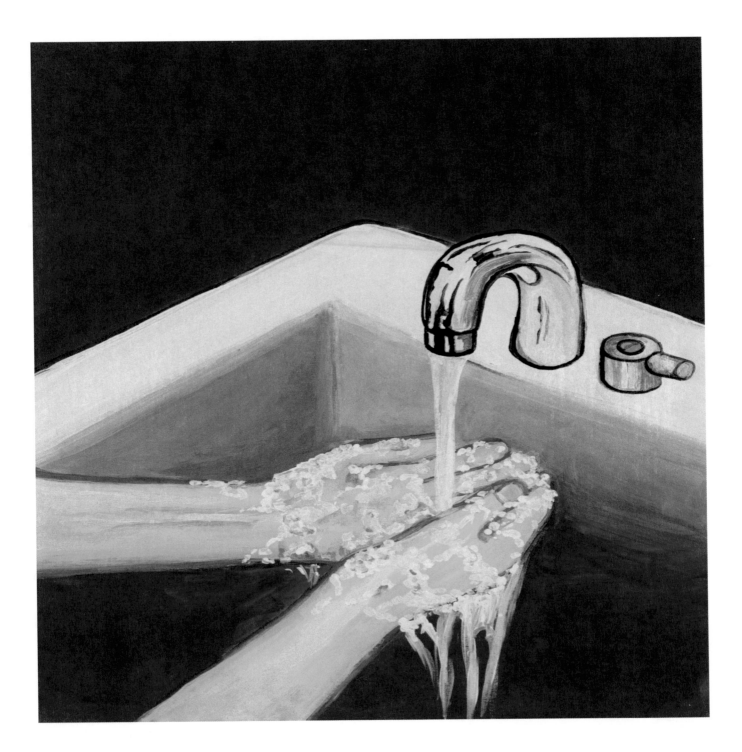

Use soap and water to get a good scrub.

Put your hands together and rub, rub, rub!

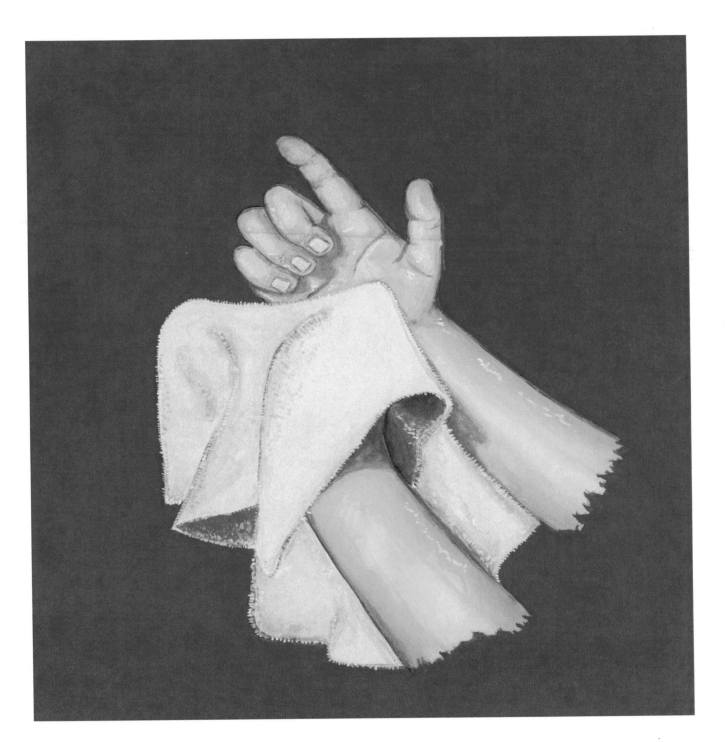

After washing your hands,
use a towel to dry.

Tell those yucky germs
goodbye.

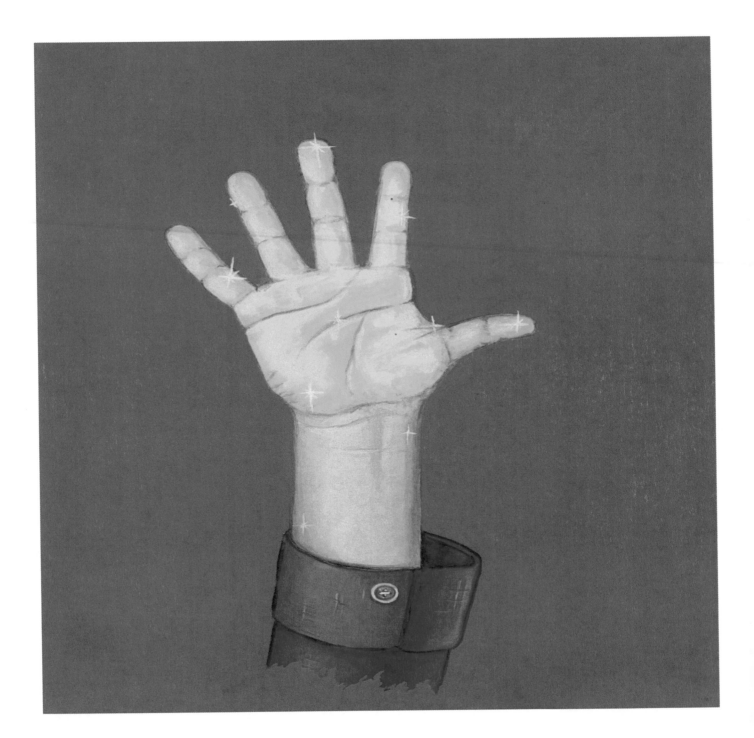

Washing your hands is the very best way to stay healthy, safe, and keep the germs away!

Active Learning Guide

• Read the book aloud. Take turns holding and turning the pages.

•Take turns describing each picture aloud. Ask questions to see what your child remembers from the story.

• Read the book before handwashing or grab a bar of soap and a washcloth to actively follow along.

•Create a daily handwashing chart or schedule.

• Give positive reinforcement for proper hygiene practices.

• Reinforce hygiene practices with verses from the book such as "Use water and soap to get a good scrub... Rub rub rub" and "Cough into your elbow please".

• Integrate the use of a favorite song to promote at least 30 seconds of hand scrubbing.

• Use a foot stool, water spout extender, scented soap or a fun washcloth to encouage fun and independence with handwashing.

Made in the USA
Middletown, DE
13 July 2022